101 Computing Challenges

Boost your programming skills

Philippe Kerampran

101 Computing

About the Author

Philippe Kerampran has worked as an ICT & Computing teacher in a UK comprehensive High School/Academy & 6th Form Centre since 2006. As a Head of Department he has introduced a computing curriculum and computing courses at GCSE and A Level. He is passionate about finding ways to share his enjoyment of computing with students while developing their abilities to become independent and resourceful learners.

Acknowledgements

To Devona, Don and Chris for their insightful feedback and for their editing and proofreading contributions.

Copyright © 2014 by 101 Computing

First Printing: 2014

ISBN: 978-1-291-91808-3

Published by:

101 Computing
Email: info@101Computing.net
Website: www.101Computing.net

Picture Credits:
Microsoft Office Clip Art Library - http://office.com
Public Domain pictures from Wikimedia Commons - http://commons.wikimedia.org

Ordering Information:
Special discounts are available on quantity purchases by corporations, associations, educators, and others. For details, contact the publisher at info@101Computing.net.

Introduction

This book is targeted at both learners (from 9 to 99 years old and above) and educators (parents, teachers) who want to adopt a challenging and enthusing approach towards learning about computing concepts whilst developing their programming skills.

As a learner...

As a learner you will be able to pick up any challenge based on topics that motivate you and match your current skills. Each challenge has a level of difficulty to help you choose. The learning objectives are clearly identified so that you can focus on a challenge based on the skills that you want to develop.

Be aware, as a learner this book does not provide you with the solution to any of the challenges. It invites you to do some research on the Internet before completing a challenge. There are "zillions" of resources on the Internet including dedicated programming websites, online communities and discussion forums, video tutorials and eBooks for you to find out and use to develop your programming knowledge.

Sometimes you will even find on the Internet the full source code for some of these challenges . There is nothing wrong in you reusing this code. On the contrary, if you dissect this code and reverse engineer it, you will really learn how the code works and you will acquire new techniques, programming habits and shortcuts from the code developed by others. This can only be positive for your own learning!

Finally, you will find more resources on our blog, www.101computing.net, as well as a "Questions & Answers" area of the website to ask questions in case you are stuck with your code and need some extra help or guidance.

You will find out that this book focuses on 5 different technologies:

⇒ HTML / CSS Challenges (with sometimes a touch of JavaScript): You will love creating your first webpages and adapting your HTML and CSS code to enhance their look & feel. You will create hyperlinks, insert pictures and add some cool interactive elements and widgets to make your webpages more dynamic.

⇒ JavaScript Challenges: These challenges will also require you to create webpages using HTML and CSS but the main focus will reside in the JavaScript code more than the actual HTML and CSS code. JavaScript code will enable you to create webpages and web-based games that interact with the end-user.

⇒ Python Challenges: You will enjoy discovering the functionalities and characteristics of this programming language. It is the perfect language to start learning how to code. Don't be fooled: this language is not just used for education purposes. It is also widely used in the IT sector to create desktop applications, mobile apps and server side scripts for web-based applications.

⇒ Scratch Challenges: Scratch is simply fantastic and I have yet to meet a learner who has not enjoyed using Scratch! With its drag and drop user interface you can build up complex video games in just a few minutes, without worrying about the syntax of your code! You will be surprised, Scratch is very flexible and enables you to create very different types of video/arcade games: "Pong like games", car racing games, platform games etc. The possibilities are endless. Scratch is not only a programming language, it's also an online community where members upload their projects. So whenever you are stuck just head to the online community, you will most certainly find someone who has already completed a similar game and be able to dissect their code to reuse and apply it to your projects.

⇒ Database Challenges: Most websites and IT systems have to store and retrieve information. Any good programmer needs some database skills! These projects will invite you to find out more about how data is stored in a relational database. You will also learn about SQL, a language used to manipulate, filter and sort data stored in databases.

As an educator/teacher...

For educators, this book can be used in many different ways. You may be running a computing club and want to find exciting challenges for students to complete together or compete against each other. Alternatively you can decide to focus on one of these challenges with your class and approach it with a more directed step by step approach to help pupils discover new skills. You can also use some of these challenges as homework tasks. Why not give students one or two of these challenges to focus on during the end of term break?

You will probably realise, whilst teaching larger groups, that the ability of students to grasp computing concepts will vary widely. This is why we believe you should allow for some differentiation by selecting different challenges for different learners based on their abilities. The main philosophy behind this book is to **challenge rather than instruct.** For learners to become good computer scientists they need to be able to acquire new skills by themselves. Do not give them the solution, do not give them too many step by step instructions (just enough to get them started). Instead encourage them to use Google. There are billions of resources on the Internet and learners need to be able to use the Internet effectively to acquire new skills and become independent learners. When learners are really stuck, encourage them to work collaboratively, to review and discuss each others' code. If they are still stuck, encourage them to look at their previous projects or point them in the right direction towards an online resource that may help them get unstuck. Focus on the process more than the actual outcome. If your learners become **more independent and resourceful learners** then praise yourself for being a fantastic teacher!

Resources

Before getting started with your first challenge you should take the time to read through the next few pages. You may have to install some software before being in a position to write any lines of code. But don't worry, we are only recommending free software so you won't need to buy anything!

Make sure you follow our recommendations as having the right tools will save you a lot of time!

In the next few pages we will be looking at:

⇒   Text Editors (e.g. Notepad ++)

⇒   Web Browsers (e.g. Mozilla Firefox or Google Chrome)

⇒   Graphic Editing Software (e.g. Paint.Net)

⇒   Python Programming Language

⇒   Python IDE (e.g. PyScripter)

⇒   PyGame Library

⇒   Scratch (Online and/or desktop application)

⇒   Desktop Relational Database Management System (e.g. Apache OpenOffice Base)

⇒   Search Engines (e.g. Google)

Notepad ++

A text-editor will be required for you to type your code, especially when writing HTML, CSS or JavaScript code. Our recommendation is to use a free text editor such as Notepad++. There are other alternatives that would most likely be suitable. When choosing your text editor you should choose one that has at least the following features:

⇒   Can edit multiple documents at the same time (e.g. using tabs)

⇒   Syntax highlighting supporting multiple programming languages (incl. HTML, CSS, JavaScript, Python)

⇒   Syntax folding (sections of code can be collapsed/expanded)

⇒   Line numbering (makes troubleshooting a lot easier)

⇒   Customizable GUI (e.g. Toolbar options, layout, colour scheme)

You can download Notepad++ for free from:

<u>http://notepad-plus-plus.org</u>

Web Browsers: Which one to go for?

To preview and test your HTML pages you will need a web browser. You most likely already have one installed on your computer. However, it's good practice to test your HTML, CSS and JavaScript projects on different web browsers. You will find out that sometimes the code you have written may not be fully compatible with all browsers or may be interpreted differently on different browsers. For desktops and laptops the most widely used web browsers are (in alphabetical order)

 ⇒   Google Chrome

⇒   Microsoft Internet Explorer

⇒   Mozilla Firefox

⇒   Opera

⇒   Safari

As more and more people are using mobile devices (smart phones, tablets), some more recent web browsers are becoming more popular.

For the purpose of the challenges presented in this book you should not worry too much though. Try to have access to at least two of the web browsers mentioned above for testing purposes.

You may also find that some of these browsers offer built-in developer tools and debugging options which can be quite handy to debug HTML, CSS and JavaScript code.

Paint.Net

When working on web-based projects and on computer games you will have to create your own graphics or manipulate existing graphics or photographs. You may have to resize or crop pictures, combine pictures, create photo montages and so on. There are many graphic editing software packages available including Adobe Photoshop, Adobe Illustrator (for vector-based graphics), Gimp, CorelDraw, Paint.Net and many more.

If you already have one of these graphic editing software packages (other than MS Paint!) then you probably do not need to install anything else. Otherwise, provided that you are on a Windows Operating System, we recommend Paint.Net, because it's free to download and has all the functionalities you will need to complete these challenges. It supports layers, various file formats and transparency. It can be used for photo editing and graphic editing and offers a fairly intuitive user interface. So all together it's a very good alternative to other costly graphic editing packages!

You can find out more and download Paint.net for free from this website:

http://www.getpaint.net/

Python & PyScripter

Python is a free to use (open-source) programming language. It is very popular as it has an easy syntax but remains quite powerful. It is used in education to teach computing concepts and programming skills and is also used in many application domains. Quite a few websites use Python such as YouTube.com which was developed in Python. Python is also popular for App development.

There are significant differences between Python 2.7 and Python 3.0 so before completing any of these Python challenges, we recommend that you download the latest version of Python for free from the Python website:

http://www.python.org

Though you can start writing and testing your own programs once you have installed Python, we would strongly recommend that you investigate installing a Python IDE (Integrated Development Environment). There are several free Python IDEs available, but if you are not sure which one to choose from, we shall recommend PyScripter which is a free, open-source IDE. It will make it a lot easier to type your code (e.g. syntax highlighting and checking as you type, indentation options) and mainly to troubleshoot and debug your code using the built-in debugging tools (e.g. breakpoints, variables windows).

You can download PyScripter for free from this webpage:

https://code.google.com/p/pyscripter/

An open-source Python Integrated Development Environment (IDE)

PyGame

After completing the first few challenges in Python you are most likely going to be eager to complete some arcade games. These will rely on a Graphical User Interface. With Python you can import libraries that will enable you to create and interact with the Graphical User Interface. We definitely recommend that you install the PyGame library which will enable you to do the following:

- ⇒ Open a new window
- ⇒ Create shapes
- ⇒ Use bitmap images
- ⇒ Add animations
- ⇒ Interact with the end-users keyboard and mouse
- ⇒ Add sound to your projects
- ⇒ Detect when objects collide

Before using the PyGame library in your code you will first have to download and install it on your own computer. You can download the latest version of the PyGame library on this website:

http://www.pygame.org

Once installed, make sure that your Python scripts start with the following code:

```
# Import the PyGame library and initialise the game engine
import pygame
pygame.init()
```

You will find plenty of tutorials on the Internet on how to use the PyGame library to create the user interface for your project.

Scratch (Online vs. desktop application)

Scratch is a free programming language and online community where you can create your own interactive stories, video games, and animations. It provides a dynamic and visual approach to programming where learners can drag and drop scripting blocks to write their computer programs. It's very popular in schools as it provides a very intuitive user interface and the ability to get started easily and to start creating complex algorithms quite quickly.

There are two options when using Scratch. You can create an account online and then use the web interface to create, save and share your games. Alternatively you can download the desktop application (Scratch 1.4 or Scratch 2.0 beta, though you may want to check the Scratch website as there might be a later version available by the time your read this book).

Find out more about Scratch on:

http://scratch.mit.edu/

MS Access or Alternative

Eight of the challenges listed in this book require you to use a RDBMS (Relational Database Management Software) package which supports the creation of multiple objects such as tables, queries, input forms and reports.

One of the most popular desktop database management systems available is Microsoft Access which is perfectly fine to complete these challenges. It's a very good tool to learn Relational Database concepts, however it is part of the Microsoft Office suite and is not free to download.

You can however consider a free alternative to Microsoft Access such as Apache OpenOffice Base. Apache OpenOffice is an open source suite of applications similar in many ways to Microsoft Office. The main difference being that it is free to download. You can find out more about Apache OpenOffice Base by visiting this webpage:

http://www.openoffice.org/product/base.html

Google, YouTube...

The most useful tool when you want to learn about programming and to complete these 101 challenges is a good **search engine**. Google or alternative search engines are the developer's best friends! Make sure you always have a window showing your search engine. Whenever you are stuck, or you can't remember the syntax of an instruction, or you are not sure if there is an HTML tag for ..., or a JavaScript command for ..., just **Google it**!

"HTML tag for ...."

"JavaScript how to ...."

"Python syntax for ...."

"CSS tutorial on..."

"Scratch video clip on how to...."

You will soon find some websites that you really like, or find useful. If you like watching "how to" **video clips** to solve problems then searching **YouTube** would be a great option. Make sure you **bookmark** your favourite websites to be able to come back to these at a later stage.

You may also find that some coders have already completed these challenges before you. You may want to download their code and try to **reverse engineer** it (take it to pieces, understand how it's made). The Scratch community for instance lets you "see the code inside" of thousands of members' projects.

http://www.google.com

Table of Content

Though we do recommend one programming language for each challenge, you can also mix these and challenge yourself using a different programming language. For instance you will find out that most JavaScript and most Scratch challenges could also be completed in Python (using the PyGame library to build the user interface).

17

Hello World!

Challenge #1

Computing Challenge

<u>Step 1</u>: Create a webpage or a computer program that displays the message "Hello World!"

<u>Step 2</u>: Adapt your script to prompt the user to enter their firstname (e.g. John).

The program should then display the following greeting:

"Hello John!"

Context:

Almost every programmer starts a new computing project with "Hello World".

Learning Objectives:

By completing this project you will learn how to get started. You will get used to the tools you will use to develop and test your projects and discover the key syntax for your programming language.

For nearly all your computing projects you will have to be able to retrieve user inputs, store values using variables and display a message as an output. This is exactly what this project will get you to do!

Level of Difficulty: **beginner**

Had a look ☐   Work in progress ☐   Nailed it! ☐

My First HTML Page!

Context:

For all your HTML and JavaScript projects you will need to start with a blank webpage. This project will show you how to get started to setup your first webpage!

Learning Objectives:

By Completing this project you will learn how to structure a webpage. You will learn how to use the <HTML>, <HEAD>, <TITLE> and <BODY> tags.

You will also understand the need to use a <STYLE> tag when including CSS code and a <SCRIPT> tag when using JavaScript code.

Lastly you will learn how to save your file using the correct file extension: ".html" for a webpage.

```
<HTML>
<HEAD>
    <TITLE>My First HTML page</TITLE>
    <STYLE>
    /*Your CSS code will go here*/

    </STYLE>
</HEAD>
<BODY>

    <H1>My First Page</H1>
    <P>Yes! This challenge is now complete</P>

</BODY>
</HTML>
```

Computing Challenge

Using a text editor (e.g. NotePad++) copy the following code. Save your file as "index.html". Open this file in your web browser.

Remember: Whenever you update your code you will need to save your changes and then refresh the page in your browser window.

Level of Difficulty: **beginner**

10-Tag Challenge

Challenge #3

Computing Challenge

Create a webpage about yourself, your hobbies or interests. Use all of the following tags and change their attributes accordingly.

<B>...</B>

<I>...</I>   <CENTER>...</CENTER>

    <FONT COLOR="red">...</FONT>

<IMG SRC="MyPicture.png" Width="100"/>   <U>...</U>

    <A HREF="http://www.101computing.net">...</A>

    <H1>...</H1>   <UL><LI>...</LI><LI>...</LI></UL>

Level of Difficulty: **beginner** ★

Learning Objectives:
You will learn how to use some of the most common HTML tags and find out about some of their attributes.

Tip:
If you want to learn more about all the HTML tags available, and their attributes, do some research on the Internet!

Did You Know?
Most tags have an opening and a closing tag such as <B> ... </B>.

For some tags however both the opening and closing tags are combined into one tag. For instance <BR/>. Did you notice the difference between these tags and where the / is located?

Had a look ☐   Work in progress ☐   Nailed it! ☐

Challenge #4

My Timetable

Learning Objectives:

You will learn how to create tables in HTML using the TABLE, TR and TD tags. You may also investigate the THEAD, TH and TBODY tags.

You will use tags' attributes and/or CSS attributes to format the different cells of your table.

Tip:

Do you know the difference between margins and padding? Do some research online to further improve the look and feel of your timetable.

Did You Know?

You can use the ROWSPAN and COLSPAN attributes of the TD tag to merge cells together.

Computing Challenge

Create a webpage to display your weekly timetable.

You will need to use a TABLE tag in HTML and think about the number of Rows and Columns you will need to complete your timetable. You can then colour-code each cell using a different colour for each subject.

★

Level of Difficulty: **beginner**

My Online Survey

Challenge
#5

Computing Challenge

Create a webpage with an online survey form. The form should ask up to ten questions using a range of form controls including:

⇒ Textboxes

⇒ Checkboxes

⇒ Radio Buttons

⇒ Drop Down Lists

⇒ Multiline Textareas

⇒ Reset Button

⇒ Submit button

Level of Difficulty: **beginner** ★

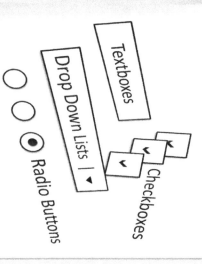

Textboxes

Drop Down Lists | ▼

Checkboxes

○ ○ ◉ Radio Buttons

Context:
Online forms are used to collect data from the end-user. They use different types of form controls including textboxes, checkboxes, radio buttons, dropdown lists, multiline textareas and buttons.

Learning Objectives:
You will learn the HTML tags used to create web-based forms using a range of form controls.

Extension:
Investigate the different attributes of form controls to add default values, select a specific option in a dropdown list, tick a checkbox or a radio button.

My Photo Collage

Challenge #6

Computing Challenge

Select five to ten pictures of your choice. Add them to a new webpage and use absolute positioning in CSS to create a photo collage. You will need to use the "position", "top", "left" and the "z-index" attributes in CSS. You could also add borders and shadow effects to your pictures.

Level of Difficulty: **beginner** ★

Context:

A picture is worth a thousand words! Pictures are an essential ingredient of most webpages. On a webpage you must use picture formats that all computers can read. This is why nearly all the pictures found on the web are .png, .jpg or .gif.

Did You Know?

PNG files and Gif files can support transparency but JPEG pictures cannot.

Learning Objectives:

You will learn how to insert pictures on a webpage using the IMG tag. You will investigate CSS positioning to place pictures next to each other or on top of each other using absolute positioning and z-index.

Where on the Map?

Challenge #7

Computing Challenge

Find a map of your town, county, country or the world. Insert it into a new webpage.

Use absolute positioning to place a pin on each location you have visited.

Add a tooltip note next to each pin to identify, or write about its location.

Level of Difficulty: **beginner** ★

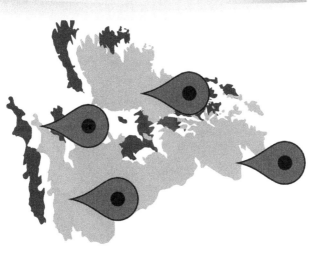

Context:
Every web-designer needs good Graphic Editing Software to create their own graphics or edit existing pictures to use on their webpages.

Learning Objectives:
You will learn about the need to edit pictures before reusing them (e.g. to resize and/or crop a section of a map).

You will understand the need to store graphics in your website folder (preferably using a "Pictures" subfolder) using meaningful filenames.

You will use absolute positioning in CSS to place the pins exactly where you want them to be on the map.

Had a look ☐   Work in progress ☐   Nailed it! ☐

Challenge #8

My FavIcon.ico

Context:

In the previous two challenges you will have learnt that pictures used on websites are most likely to be PNG, JPEG or GIF files.

Favicons are another type of graphic that can be used on the web. They will not be used within the content of a webpage but instead will appear in the address bar of your web-browser or, when your page is bookmarked, its favicon will appear to make your page stand out in your list of bookmarks.

Learning Objectives:

You will learn the purpose of favicon.ico files, how to create them using an online favicon generator and how to use HTML to attach them to your page.

Computing Challenge

Find an online favicon generator to create a favicon to use on one of your own webpages. Download the icon you have created and add the HTML code to make sure it displays properly as a favicon on your web-browser's address bar.

Level of Difficulty: **beginner** ★

Had a look ☐   Work in progress ☐   Nailed it! ☐

Bookmark Me!

Computing Challenge

Create a webpage on which you are going to add a link that enables the end-user to bookmark your webpage (add to their favourites). You will need to find a script online to do this. Try to find a script that checks for the type of browser being used and ensure it will work with most browsers.

Level of Difficulty: **beginner** ★

Context:
While searching the web you will find some websites particularly useful and will want to remember how to access them quickly. An easy way to do so is to "bookmark" them (add them to your favourites or to your favourites bar), so that you can quickly go back to these sites in the future.

Learning Objectives:
You are going to learn how to create a hyperlink that, once clicked, will add your webpage to the end-user's browser list of favourites. To do so you will have to use a bit of JavaScript code that you will find online.

You will test your code using different web-browsers to see if it works.

Had a look ☐   Work in progress ☐   Nailed it! ☐

Challenge #10

My Popups

Computing Challenge

Create a webpage with links to all your HTML, CSS and JavaScript projects. Each project should open in its own popup window. For each link/popup you decide what size of popup you want (width and height), whether it needs a toolbar, menubar, status bar and scrollbars. The popup window should appear in the middle of the screen.

Level of Difficulty: **beginner** ★

Context:

When building a webpage you can add some JavaScript code that can interact with various objects of your webpage such as headings, form controls etc. All these objects are accessible in JavaScript using the DOM (Document Object Model) that lists all of the objects that can be used and all of their attributes and methods.

The browser window itself is an object that you can manipulate in JavaScript.

Learning Objectives:

You will learn how to create hyperlinks to other webpages and make these hyperlinks open in different windows. Using JavaScript you will change the parameters of these

Web Clock

Computing Challenge

Find a script online to create a clock on your webpage which will display the current time.

You may display the time using an analogue clock or a digital clock.

Learning Objectives:
You will develop your ability to search the web and find existing scripts that you can adapt and reuse in your own project.

Tips:
The first script you find on the web may not be the best one. Try to find several scripts and compare their features. Also, be aware that scripts that you find on the web may be copyrighted. Make sure you check to see whether you can re-use the script or not.

Finally, you may find scripts that only work with some but not all web-browsers. Try to find a script that is compatible with the main web-browsers.

Level of Difficulty: **beginner** ★

Had a look ☐   Work in progress ☐   Nailed it! ☐

My Widgets

Did You Know?

There are thousands of free widgets to use on the Internet. The most popular ones are the Google Maps widget, various weather forecasting widgets and social networks feeds such as Twitter or Facebook feeds.

These are very easy to integrate into an existing website. Sometimes though they need to be customised in terms of dimensions and look and feel options so that they don't ruin the look and feel of your website.

Learning Objectives:

You will learn how to integrate two of the most popular widgets: Google Maps and Weather Forecast to an existing webpage.

London—UK

Monday	3°C	
Tuesday	4°C	
Wednesday	4°C	
Thursday	1°C	
Friday	-1°C	

Computing Challenge

Create a webpage about your school. Find a widget online to display on your page the current weather with a five-day weather forecast in the town/city where your school is based.

Add a Google map widget to show how to get to your school.

Level of Difficulty: **beginner** ★

My CSS Layout

Computing Challenge

Create a webpage with the following layout (see diagram below). Each area should be defined using DIV tags and CSS, without using any table!

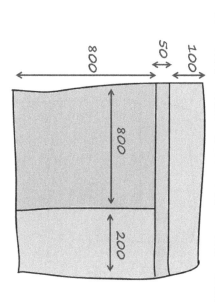

Context:
One of the key elements of a successful webpage is its layout. A clear, well-thought layout will make your website easy-to-use and look professional and well balanced!

Though some web-developers used to create websites using HTML tables it is not recommended anymore. Instead the layout of a website should be implemented in CSS.

Learning Objectives:
You will learn how to create a simple webpage layout using CSS.

Tip:
On the diagram, the dimensions are given in pixels (px).

Level of Difficulty: **intermediate** ★ ★

Had a look ☐   Work in progress ☐   Nailed it! ☐

Challenge #14

Responsive CSS Layout

Context:

As more and more users access the Internet via smaller devices (e.g. smartphones) it is required to design websites that can have mobile phone friendly layouts.

A website that has a layout that changes based on the size of the screen is called a responsive website.

Learning Objectives:

You will learn how to use CSS to create a responsive layout that adapts to the size of the end-user's screen.

Tip:

You can test your website by resizing the browser window to see how it will adapt to a small window/screen.

100
50
800

200
800

Computing Challenge

Adapt the layout from the previous challenge so that when the page is viewed in a smaller window (<1000px wide) the layout automatically changes, as shown on the right.

This will be a better layout for mobile phone users.

★
★ ★
★ ★ ★

Level of Difficulty: **advanced**

My CSS Text Frames

Challenge #15

Computing Challenge

Create a new webpage with your favourite inspirational quotes. Each quote should appear in a text frame (using DIV tags).

Use CSS to format each text frame. Investigate using padding, margins, borders, rounded corners, shadow, background effects (picture, colour, gradient). Format the text too using various font options, line spacing, character spacing and text alignment.

Level of Difficulty: **intermediate** ★ ★ ★

Context:
The two main purposes of CSS are to firstly create page layouts (as seen in previous challenges) and secondly to format text, pictures and other objects on the page.

Learning Objectives:
You will investigate various CSS properties to format text (font size, type, colour, weight etc.) and text frames (using borders, padding, margins, background colours, gradients or pictures).

Did You Know?
When using background pictures for webpages or text frames, you can use smaller pictures that will repeat either horizontally, vertically or both to create a pattern. This is called tiling!

My Tabs

Challenge #16

Did You Know?

When creating webpages you can use HTML tags, CSS code and JavaScript code. The mix of these three languages is called DHTML (Dynamic HTML) as it enables you to create more interactive webpages.

Learning Objectives:

You will use DHTML (HTML + CSS + JavaScript) to create some dynamic tabs.

Tip:

You may want to find a script online to see how it works. You can also investigate the "display: block;" or "display: none;" CSS declarations to show or hide content on your webpage.

Computing Challenge

Create a new webpage about any topic in which you are interested. (Why not a page about you?) Add three horizontal tabs that the user can click on to reveal the content of the tab. When a tab is clicked the content of the other tabs should be hidden.

About Me	My Music	My Pictures

Some text and pictures....

Level of Difficulty: **intermediate** ★★

Roll-Over QR Codes

Had a look ☐   Work in progress ☐   Nailed it! ☐

Computing Challenge

Create a webpage displaying the logo of at least three of your favourite brands or websites.

When the user rolls over one of the logos a QR code appears in place of the logo.

Level of Difficulty: **intermediate** ★★

101 Computing

Context:
Roll-over effects are often used on the web to indicate that a picture is clickable. They can for instance be used as buttons in a navigation bar.

Did You Know:
You can easily create your own QR codes. To do so type "QR code generator" in Google. You will find a website where you can enter a web address (URL) to generate the matching QR Code.

Learning Objectives:
You will learn how to create your own QR codes and use the onMouseOver, onMouseOut events of the IMG tags.

Had a look ☐   Work in progress ☐   Nailed it! ☐

Challenge #18

My School Map

Did You Know?

An image map is a picture on a webpage that has different sections that are clickable. It can be used to set up a graphical menu or to make sections of a chart link to other pages of a website.

Learning Objectives:

You will learn how to create an image map as an alternative method to navigate through a website or link towards external webpages.

Tip:

The web address of a webpage is also called the URL. It often starts with http:// (or https:// for secure/encrypted webpages)

Computing Challenge

Find an aerial picture of your school on the Internet (e.g. Google Maps)

Create a webpage with an **image map** so that when you click on a specific building of your school it links to the right department page on your school website or VLE.

Level of Difficulty: **intermediate**

Had a look ☐ Work in progress ☐ Nailed it! ☐

Splash Screen

Computing Challenge

Find a script online to create a Splash Screen for your webpage.

Customise the script so that the splash screen only appears for three seconds.

Extension: Your splash screen should be different based on the end-user's screen size!

Level of Difficulty: **intermediate** ★★

Context:
Webpages are accessed from a wide range of computer and mobile devices. The best websites use a responsive design where the content, look and feel and functionalities vary based on the size of the end-user's screen.

Learning Objectives:
You will understand the need to adapt the content of a webpage based on the size of the screen and the screen resolution of the end-user.

You will investigate methods that can be used to detect the size of the end-user's screen before choosing what content (splash screen) to reveal.

Had a look ☐   Work in progress ☐   Nailed it! ☐

Challenge #20

Quote Scroller

Computing Challenge

Find a script online to create a text scroller on your webpage.

The scroller should display your favourite inspirational quotes.

The text will scroll either horizontally or vertically.

Level of Difficulty: **advanced**

Computing Challenge

Find a script online to create a text scroller on your webpage.

The scroller should display your favourite inspirational quotes.

The text will scroll either horizontally or vertically.

Context:

Why re-invent the wheel? Very often programmers have to reuse existing modules or blocks of codes written by someone else. They can then amend or tweak the code to meet their own requirements.

Learning Objectives:

You will develop your ability to search the web and find existing scripts that you can adapt and reuse in your own project.

Extension:

Customise your script: Can you change the background and the text colour, the speed of the scrolling effect, the direction of the scrolling effect? Can you make it loop (start again when it reaches the end of the text)?

My Image Gallery

Computing Challenge

Find a script online to create an interactive picture gallery.

Customise the script to display your own set of pictures.

Level of Difficulty: **advanced** ★ ★ ★

Context:

You will find plenty of image gallery scripts online . Find a few that you like and compare their features. Investigate how easy they are to customise. Try them on different web browsers such as Internet Explorer, Firefox, Google Chrome. Also, try them on a tablet or smartphone to see if they work.

Learning Objectives:

You will understand the various criteria to take into consideration when choosing a script online: How easy is it to customise? Is it compatible with the main web browsers and with touchscreens (Tablets and smartphones)? Is it easy to reuse? Is it fully documented?

Pull-Down Menus

Challenge #22

Context:

Most websites will make use of a navigation bar. Sometimes the navigation bar will include various levels of navigation with pull down menus.

Learning Objectives:

You will develop your ability to search the web and find existing scripts that you can adapt and reuse in your own projects. You will also find out that some scripts may not be fully compatible with all web browsers and devices including tablets and smart phones.

Tip:

Find a script that is compatible with most web browsers. Also test your script on a touchscreen/tablet.

Computing Challenge

Find a script online to create a pull-down menu on your webpage.

Customise the script so that your pull down menu displays links towards other pages of your site or towards your favourite websites.

HOME	MY COMPUTING PROJECTS ▾	MY LINKS

HTML / CSS

JavaScript

Python

Level of Difficulty: **advanced** ★★★

Google Fonts

Computing Challenge

Create a webpage about a topic in which you are interested.

Select one or more fonts from the Google Fonts page:

https://www.google.com/fonts

Apply these fonts to your webpage.

Level of Difficulty: **advanced** ★★★

Did You Know?

When designing a webpage you have to be very careful about the fonts you decide to use. If you use some fancy fonts that are installed on your computer, you have no guarantee these fonts will be available on other internet users' computers. So most websites stick to the widely used fonts such as Arial, Times New Roman, Verdana etc. If you want to use fancier fonts you may consider using Google Fonts as these will be made available to all.

Learning Objectives:

You will understand the need to be cautious when choosing a font when designing a website and learn how to apply a Google Font to your own webpage.

Had a look ☐ Work in progress ☐ Nailed it! ☐

My Colour Palette

Click on a colour to change the page background!

Did You Know?

When designing a webpage or working with computer graphics, each colour has a unique code which is called an hexadecimal code. For example the hexadecimal code for black is #000000 and the code for white is #FFFFFF

Learning Objectives:

You will learn about hexadecimal colour codes. You will learn how JavaScript can interact with some HTML tags to change their attributes. (For instance to change the BGColor attribute of the BODY tag).

Watch Out:

When using HTML the word "colour" (English spelling) is spelt "color" (American spelling).

Computing Challenge

Create an HTML page where the end-user can change the background colour of the page by clicking on a colour palette.

Level of Difficulty: **beginner**

Guess the Colour

Computing Challenge

Create an HTML page where a random colour code is displayed in #hex format. The page then displays 14 buttons of different colours. The user needs to guess the matching colour by clicking on the correct button. If the user is incorrect a message will invite him to try again.

Level of Difficulty: **beginner** ★

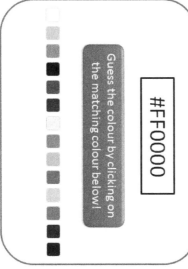

Guess the colour by clicking on the matching colour below!

#FF0000

Did You Know?

Each colour is made of a unique combination of Reg, Green and Blue.

When using colours in HTML, you can either use the name of the colour (e.g. "red") or their RGB code (e.g. rgb(255,0,0)) or their hexadeximal code (e.g. #FF0000).

Learning Objectives:

You will learn about hexadecimal colour codes and RGB colour codes.

Challenge
#26

What's the Time

In New-York?

New York - AM

London - PM

Los Angeles - AM

Paris - PM

Computing Challenge

Create a webpage that tells the end user the current time in different locations: London, Paris, Sydney, New-York, Tokyo.

Context:
Websites can be viewed by Internet users located all around the world. Using JavaScript you can retrieve the current time of their computer and find out their time zone.

Learning Objectives:
You will learn how to manipulate date and time functions to identify the end-user's time zone, and add or subtract a given number of hours to the current time.

Extension:
You may find a script online to display the time using an analogue clock.

Level of Difficulty: **beginner** ★

Christmas Countdown

Computing Challenge

Write a little program that tells the end-user how many days are left until next Christmas.

**12 Days
'Til
Christmas**

Learning Objectives:
By completing this project you will learn how to manipulate dates and use date functions.

Extension:
Will your program still work next year and the year after next?

Tip:
Once you have completed this program, type "Christmas Countdown" into Google to compare your outcome with an online Christmas Countdown website.

Had a look ☐ Work in progress ☐ Nailed it! ☐

Daily Greetings

Computing Challenge

Create a webpage that displays the correct greeting based on the time of the day:

⇑ Good Morning (Between 6:01 and 12:00)

⇑ Good Afternoon (Between 12:01 and 18:00)

⇑ Good Evening (Between 18.01 and 21:00)

⇑ Good Night (Between 21:01 and 6:00)

Bonjour!

Learning Objectives:

You will learn how to use date and time functions to retrieve the current time (as set on the end-user's computer). Then you will use conditional "if statements" to display the relevant greeting.

Extension:

Using JavaScript you can find the language of the end-user's web browser. You could use this information to display these greetings in different languages such as French or Spanish.

Level of Difficulty: beginner

Quote of the Day

Had a look ☐   Work in progress ☐   Nailed it! ☐

Computing Challenge

Create a webpage that displays a different quote every time it is loaded/refreshed.

Add a button to let the end-user change the quote automatically.

Quote of the Day

"A JPEG is worth a thousand words"

Get New Quote

Learning Objectives:

You will learn how JavaScript can be used to amend the content of a webpage.

Alternative Approaches:

You will either use the DOM to access objects on the page and change their properties (e.g. using the *innerHTML* property).

Alternatively you may use inline javaScript code, directly embedded within the HTML code to write content when the page is loaded using the *document.write* instruction.

Word Count

Computing Challenge

Create a webpage with a textarea.

The end-users should be able to type or copy some text.

The webpage should automatically indicate the number of words contained in the textarea.

Did You Know?
When using Twitter you can only type tweets of 140 characters max. This task is different though as it is asking for a total number of words instead of characters.

Learning Objectives:
You will learn about string manipulation techniques and how text/strings can be stored as arrays.

Tip:
You may want to investigate how the split function works to convert a string into an array. You will then find a way to retrieve the length of the array.

Word Count

Type some text:

Coding is fun. Everyone should have a go at coding their own computer programs.

Word Count: 14

Level of Difficulty: **beginner**

JavaScript

Had a look ☐   Work in progress ☐   Nailed it! ☐

On Which Day of the Week Were You Born?

Monday
Tuesday
Wednesday
Thursday
Friday
Saturday
Sunday

Computing Challenge

Write a little program that prompts the end-user to enter their Date of Birth and which returns the day of the week on which they were born (Monday, Tuesday etc.).

Did You Know?
In European countries it is common to use the dd/mm/yyyy format when writing a date, whereas in the US the most common date format is: mm/dd/yyyy. It can become tricky if you are given a date such as 10/12/2014 and are not sure which format is used.

Learning Objectives:
By completing this project you will learn how to manipulate dates and use date functions.

Extension:
Can you add some validation rules to make sure that the user has typed a valid date in your selected format (dd/mm/yyyy or mm/dd/yyyy) and display an error message if not?

My Countdown Timer

Computing Challenge

Create a countdown timer program where the user enters a time in minutes and seconds. When they press the start button the timer will display, and constantly update, the remaining time.

Learning Objectives:

By completing this project you will learn how to use a single loop to repeat a set of instructions.

Tip:

Start by displaying the time in a digital format.

Extension:

Adapt your script to find a visual way to represent the time left. For instance you could use a progress bar.

Add a sound effect to indicate when the time has expired.

Level of Difficulty: **intermediate** ★★

JavaScript

Form Validation

Challenge #33

Computing Challenge

Create a webpage with an on-line form asking for the following fields:

Firstname, Lastname, Date of Birth, E-mail Address and Phone Number.

When the end-user clicks on the "Submit" button the page should check the user input and display an error message if one of the following is true:

⇒ Firstname or lastname is left empty,

⇒ The Date of Birth is not a date in the past,

⇒ The e-mail address does not contain an @ sign,

⇒ The Phone number is less than eleven characters long.

When all conditions are met the page should display a confirmation message.

Level of Difficulty: **intermediate** ★★

Context:

Nowadays most websites have input forms to login, subscribe to a newsletter, request a quote etc. However, end-users sometimes make mistakes (on purpose or not) when completing the form. Using form validation is a way to ensure that the data being entered complies with certain rules before being submitted.

Learning Objectives:

By completing this project you will investigate various form validation methods including presence check (required field), format check, length check (based on the number of characters being entered) and range check.

Challenge
#34

Captcha

Computing Challenge

Create a webpage with an on-line form asking for the following fields:

Firstname, Lastname, Email Address.

The page should also display a Captcha challenge based on a mathematical equation (e.g. 7+3=?).
The end-user will have to type the answer in a textbox before submitting the form.

The script should check that the end-user did get the right answer and display an error message if not.

Each time the page is reloaded, the Captcha challenge should change.

Level of Difficulty: **intermediate** ★★

Context:

Most websites have input forms to login, subscribe to a newsletter, request a quote etc. It is sometimes required to add a CAPTCHA challenge to ensure that the form is being filled in by a human being rather than a bot! Bots have been designed to automatically fill in forms, to take part in online surveys, to try to register for newsletters, to collect e-mail addresses and then send SPAM. They may also try to guess valid usernames and passwords.

Learning Objectives:

By completing this project you will learn about the purpose of CAPTCHA and be able to use a mathematical approach to create your own CAPTCHA.

Challenge
#35

Paper Size

Paper Size:

A4 | ▼

Unit:

in | cm | ▼

Dimensions:

= | 21 x 29.7

Computing Challenge

Create a webpage where the end-user can select a paper size and a unit so that the page displays the dimensions of the paper in the selected unit.

Size	Height x Width (mm)	Height x Width (in)
A0	1189 x 841 mm	46.8 x 33.1 in
A1	841 x 594 mm	33.1 x 23.4 in
A2	594 x 420 mm	23.4 x 16.5 in
A3	420 x 297 mm	16.5 x 11.7 in
A4	297 x 210 mm	11.7 x 8.3 in
A5	210 x 148 mm	8.3 x 5.8 in
A6	148 x 105 mm	5.8 x 4.1 in
A7	105 x 74 mm	4.1 x 2.9 in
A8	74 x 52 mm	2.9 x 2.0 in
A9	52 x 37 mm	2.0 x 1.5 in
A10	37 x 26 mm	1.5 x 1.0 in

Did You Know?
The international A4 paper size is slightly longer (18mm) and narrower (6mm) than the US Letter paper size. A4 is used in most countries except in the US which uses the Letter format.

Learning Objectives:
You will learn how JavaScript can interact with various form controls for instance to retrieve the selected value from a drop down list or to change the value in a textbox.

Extension:
Investigate the use of alternative form controls such as radio buttons and checkboxes to complete this task.

Level of Difficulty: **intermediate** ★★

Had a look ☐ Work in progress ☐ Nailed it! ☐

My Calculator

Challenge #36

Computing Challenge

Create a webpage that displays all the buttons that would appear on a basic calculator and that can be used to perform basic maths operations:

⇒ plus: +

⇒ minus: -

⇒ multiply: *

⇒ divide: /

Tip?
Type "Calculator" in Google to find an example of a web-based JavaScript calculator.

Learning Objectives:
You will learn how to to manipulate numbers in javascript using the basic operators: +,-,*,/

You will also understand the need to convert text values (user input) into real numbers (using the *parseFloat()* function)

Level of Difficulty: **intermediate** ★★

Challenge #37

How Secure Is Your Password?

Computing Challenge

Create a webpage or a program where the end-user has to type a password. The program should return a score to tell the end-user the security level of their password.

Type your password

myPa$$w0rd;

Your Security Score: 25pts

This is a fairly secure password. To make it even more secure you should consider:

- Adding numbers to your password

Criteria

Criteria	Score
The password is at least 8 characters long.	+5pts
The password contains number and letters.	+10pts
The password contains at least one punctuation sign.	+5pts
The password contains lowercase and uppercase characters.	+10pts

Level of Difficulty: **intermediate** ★★

Did You Know?
The most widespread form of hacking does not require any technical knowledge. It consists of reusing someone else's password. If your password is too obvious, based on actual English words, someone looking over your shoulder, when you type it, will find it easy to guess or copy.

Learning Objectives:
This project focuses on string manipulation and the use of regular expressions.

Tip:
To complete this project you will need to investigate how to use regular expressions to search for specific characters in a string.

Currency Converter

Challenge #38

Computing Challenge

Create a webpage that lets the end-user enter an amount they want to convert, as well as the currencies they want to convert from/to.

The webpage should automatically calculate the converted amount to the selected currency.

Amount   £100

in   Pounds ▶

Convert to   Euros ▶

=

€120.33

Learning Objectives:

You will learn how to manipulate real numbers and adjust the number of decimal places when required.

Tip:

Start with just 3 or 4 currencies and find their exchange rates on the Internet.

Extension:

Make sure that all results are displayed to two decimal places.

Use validation rules to ensure that the end-user only inserts valid numbers.

Level of Difficulty: intermediate ★★ ★★

How Fast Can You Type?

The quick brown fox jumps over the lazy dog.

The qui|

✗   Your time so far

7 sec

Computing Challenge

Create a webpage where the end-user has to type a sentence as quickly as they can without making any errors.

The webpage will display a random sentence that the end-user will have to type. It will then show whether the user typed it correctly or not, and how long it took to type.

Level of Difficulty: **advanced**   ★ ★ ★

Did You Know?

Touch typing consists of typing on the keyboard using all of one's fingers without looking at the keys.

Good to know:

"The quick brown fox jumps over the lazy dog" is a famous quotation used in typing because it uses every single letter of the alphabet from a to z. It is also used to show what a font looks like.

Learning Objectives:

You will learn how to use a timer in JavaScript and how to use an "if statement" to compare a user input with a predefined value. You may also use an array to store a collection of sentences for the user to type.

JavaScript

Had a look ☐   Work in progress ☐   Nailed it! ☐

Challenge #40

#Hex / RGB Colour Converter

Red   Green   Blue
255   255   255

Hex

#FFFFFF

Context:

Web designers create websites using a colour scheme based on a small selection of colours (usually 3 to 5 colours per website). They may choose these colours or have to reuse colours from an existing logo or picture.

In HTML and CSS we can use two notations to identify a colour: the RGB notation or the Hexadecimal notation. Most graphic packages will use both notations.

Learning Objectives:

To complete this project you will first need to learn how to convert hexadecimal colour codes into RGB colour codes and vice versa.

Computing Challenge

Create a program or a webpage that lets the user convert an RGB colour code in #Hex format and vice versa.

Level of Difficulty: **advanced** ★★★★★

My Texting App

Computing Challenge

Create a webpage that displays a phone screen and keypad with 12 keys (see picture).

The end-user should be able to type a message using the ABC multi-tap mode: In this mode you type a letter by pressing each key the number of times required for a particular letter on that key. For example, to type the letter b, you would press the 2 key twice because b is the second letter on that key.

Level of Difficulty: **advanced** ★★★

Context:
When designing Apps, it is important to make sure that the App will work on various mobile phone devices and tablets. These come with different screen sizes and different types of keypads or on-screen keyboards.

Learning Objectives:
You will combine HTML, CSS and JavaScript effectively to create this interactive webpage, reproducing the design of a mobile phone.

Tip:
You can either use HTML buttons or create one picture per button. Alternatively you can use an image map using one picture only (picture of a mobile phone).

JavaScript

Memory Game

Challenge #42

Computing Challenge

Create a game of Memory using a 4X4 grid of cards. All of the cards are laid face down. The player flips two cards face up for each turn. If the player finds a pair of matching cards then the two cards remain as they are (face up) otherwise they are flipped over again (face down). The game ends when all the pairs have been found.

Learning Objectives:
By completing this project you will manipulate a two-dimensional array to store the position of the cards on the grid.

Extension:
Add a timer to time how long it takes for the player to complete the grid.

Alternatively you can adapt this game to be played by one to four players. Each player takes it in turn and scores a point every time they find a pair.

Level of Difficulty: **advanced** ★ ★ ★

Tic-Tac-Toe

Challenge
#43

Computing Challenge

Create a game of Noughts & Crosses (aka Tic-Tac-Toe) where the user plays against the computer!

Level of Difficulty: **advanced**   ★ ★ ★

Learning Objectives:

You will investigate how to create a game where the user plays against the computer. To do this you may want the computer to randomly place a token on the grid. A higher level algorithm would require the computer has to test every possibility and decide which option is the best.

Tip:

Consider using a 3X3 array to store the position of noughts and crosses on the grid.

Had a look ☐   Work in progress ☐   Nailed it! ☐

Challenge
#44

Connect4

Computing Challenge

Create a game of Connect4 where the user can either play against another player or against the computer.

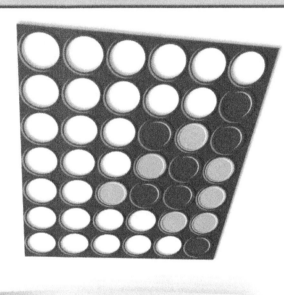

Tip:

Make sure you have completed challenge 43: Tic-Tac-Toe before completing this challenge. The approach will be very similar but this time it will be based on a 6x7 array.

Learning Objectives:

By completing this game you will apply all your DHTML skills (JavaScript, HTML and CSS) to create the graphical user interface of the game.

You will combine Loops, "if statements" and two-dimensional arrays effectively.

Extension:

You can create different levels by using different approaches for the computer to decide where to place its tokens.

Level of Difficulty: **advanced** ★★★

Hangman

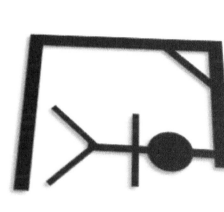

Computing Challenge

Write a little program where the user has to guess a word randomly selected by the computer. (The lists of accepted words should be stored as a text file, one word per line).

The user should enter one letter at a time and get instant feedback from the computer.

Level of Difficulty: **advanced** ★★★

Tip:
You may have issues getting JavaScript to access a text file on your computer as most web browsers' security settings would prevent JavaScript accessing the file system. However, you can bypass these restrictions by saving your webpage as an HTML application using the extension .hta instead of .html.

Learning Objectives:
You will learn how to create an HTML application (.hta) and how to open and read through a text file using JavaScript.

You May Also...
Have you considered completing this game in Python?

Had a look ☐   Work in progress ☐   Nailed it! ☐

Adding from 1 to 100

Challenge
#46

$$1+2+3+4+5+...+98+99+100 =$$

$$? ? ?$$

Computing Challenge

Use a computer algorithm to calculate the following sum:

$$1+2+3+4+5+... ...+99+100$$

Context:

There is often more than one solution to a problem. In this scenario you need to find the most effective solution.

Challenge yourself by completing this program using a minimal number of lines of code.

Learning Objectives:
You will investigate the use of loops in Python.

Extension:
Amend your code to count odd numbers only (1+3+5+7+...+97+99) or to count in 5s. (0+5+10+15+....95+100)

Level of Difficulty: **beginner** ★

My Average Score

Challenge #47

Computing Challenge

Write a little program that prompts the end-user to enter a list of numbers.

The program will calculate and display the min, max and average values from this list.

10 5 54 26 18

Level of Difficulty: **beginner** ★

Learning Objectives:
By completing this project you will learn how to use a one-dimension array (list) to append input values from the end-user.

Extension:
You can add some validation methods to ensure that the user is only typing numbers.

When calculating your average score you may end up with a decimal number. You can find out how to format a number to only show two decimal places.

Guess the Number

Challenge
#48

Computing Challenge

Write a little program that randomly picks a number between 1 and 100.

The user has to guess the number by entering different values until it guesses the exact number.

For each guess, the program should return the following feedback to the end-user:

Guess	Feedback
For any guess which is at least 50 above or below the actual number	"Not Even Close"
For any guess less than 50 above the actual number	"You are too hot"
For any guess less than 50 below the actual number	"You are too cold"
If the guess matches the actual number	"Spot on"

Level of Difficulty: **beginner** ★

Learning Objectives?

You will use comparison operators within "if statements" to compare two numbers. The main comparison operators are as follows:

== (equal to)
!= (not equal to)
< (less than)
> (greater than)
<= (less than or equal to)
>= (greater than or equal to)

Tip:

To generate random numbers you may want to import the "random" Python library by adding the following command at the beginning of your code:

import random

Prime Number Check

Level of Difficulty: **beginner** ★

Challenge #49

Computing Challenge

Write a little program that prompts the user to enter a number between 1 and 9999. The program will inform the end-user whether their number is a prime number or not.

Context:

A prime number can be divided evenly only by 1, or itself. A prime number must be a whole number greater than 1.

3, 5, 7, 11, 13, 17... are all examples of prime numbers.

Did You Know?

In computing there are two types of numbers: Integers which are whole numbers with no decimal places (such as 7) and Reals which are numbers with decimal places (such as 3.14).

Learning Objectives:

You will learn how to use loops and "if statements" to check all potential divisors of a number.

Had a look ☐   Work in progress ☐   Nailed it! ☐

Challenge
#50

Poker Dice

Computing Challenge

Create a simplified version of Poker Dice using only three dice. The player should be able to "throw the dice": the dice will randomly display a number between 1 and 6. The user scores points as follows:

⇨ Three of a Kind: +50 points

⇨ Straight (e.g. 3, 4, 5): +30 points

⇨ 3 Odd Numbers: +15 points

⇨ 3 Even Numbers: +15 points

⇨ 1 Pair: +10 points

Level of Difficulty: **beginner** ★

Learning Objectives:
By completing this project you will learn how to generate random numbers and how to create basic user interaction with the end-user.

Extension:
The player should be allowed up to three throws. After each throw the player can decide which dice to keep and which dice to throw again.

Tip:
To generate random numbers you may want to import the "random" Python library by adding the following command at the beginning of your code:
import random

What's my Age?

Computing Challenge

Write a little program that prompts the end-user to enter their date of birth.

The program should inform the end-user of their actual age in years, months and days. For instance: "You are 16 years, 6 months and 7 days old!"

Learning Objectives:
By completing this project you will learn how to manipulate date entries and use some of the Date functions.

Extension:
You could adapt your script to calculate the time left in days or hours between now and the next event of your choice (School holidays, Olympic Games, Next Solar Eclipse...)! Or you could prompt the user to enter two different dates to calculate the number of days between these two dates.

Level of Difficulty: **beginner** ★

Had a look ☐   Work in progress ☐   Nailed it! ☐

Backwards Writing
sdrawkcaB gnitirW

Challenge #52

Computing Challenge

Write a little program that lets the end-user enter a piece of text.

The program will convert the input so that every word is written backwards.

For instance the text: "backwards writing" becomes "sdrawkcab gnitirw"

Learning Objectives:

By completing this challenge you will further improve your string manipulation techniques. You will use a technique called "slicing". Do some research first to find out about the Python Slice notation.

Tip:

You may want to investigate using the "split" function to break up a string into a list. (e.g. to separate each word of the given text).

Have You Thought About?

What should you do with punctuation signs such as commas and full stops?

Level of Difficulty: **beginner** ★

Python

It's All in the Case

Computing Challenge

Write a little program that lets the end-user enter a piece of text.

The user should then be able to convert their text into the following formats:

⇒ ALL UPPERCASE

⇒ all lowercase

⇒ Title Case

⇒ Sentence case.

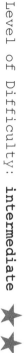

Level of Difficulty: **intermediate** ★★

Did You Know?

Most modern programming languages such as JavaScript and Python are case sensitive. This matters for instance when defining variables, and creating your own functions.

Most programmers like to follow the "Camel Case" convention when naming variables and functions. A variable in a programming language is said to be "camelCased" when all words but the first are capitalized: e.g. myFirstVariable is in camelCase.

Learning Objectives:

This project will further develop your abilities to manipulate strings using Python's built-in string functions.

Challenge
#54

Random Password Generator

Computing Challenge

Write a little program that generates a random password that matches the following security criteria.

⇒ The password will be eight to twelve characters long.

⇒ The password will include numbers and letters.

⇒ The password will include at least one punctuation sign.

⇒ The password will include lowercase and uppercase letters.

Did You Know?
Every character that you can type with your keyboard has a unique code/number. This is the purpose of the ASCII code.

Learning Objectives:
You will learn how to generate random characters by generating random ASCII codes within a range of acceptable ASCII codes.

Tip:
To generate random numbers you may want to import the "random" Python library by adding the following command at the beginning of your code:

import random

Level of Difficulty: **intermediate**

Love Match Calculator

Computing Challenge

Write a little program that prompts the user to enter two first names.

The program will return a Love Match Score based on the following criteria:

Criteria	Score
Both first names have the same number of letters.	+20pts
Both first names start with a vowel.	+10pts
Both first names start with a consonant.	+5pts
Both first names have the same number of consonants.	+12pts
Both first names have the same number of vowels.	+12pts
Both first names contain either an "i", "o", "v" or "e".	+7pts

Level of Difficulty: **intermediate** ★★

Learning Objectives:
This challenge focuses on string manipulation techniques. You will use the "string slicing" technique in Python. Make sure you do some research on the Internet first to fully understand how string slicing works in Python as it has its own specific notation.

Extension:
You could extend this project further by asking for, and comparing, dates of birth (DoB). Add to the score if both DoB are in the same year, month or day of the week (e.g. Monday to Sunday). This will further improve your date manipulation techniques.

Darts Scoreboard

Computing Challenge

Write a little program that prompts the user to enter how many points they score each time they throw a dart.

The calculator should automatically display how many points are remaining to finish the game, and finally how many throws it took to complete the game.

Level of Difficulty: **intermediate** ★★

Tip:
Not sure how points are being calculated when playing darts? Do some research on the internet to find out!

Learning Objectives:
You will use your Python skills to perform some basic mathematical operations using the input from the end-user. You will understand the need to convert user inputs into integers before using them in mathematical operations.

Extension:
Use file manipulation techniques to write the score into a text file as the game progresses so that the user can keep track of their previous games.

What's My Change?

Challenge
#57

Computing Challenge

Write a program that prompts the end-user to enter two values:

⇒ Value 1: Amount to be paid by the customer.

⇒ Value 2: Amount received from the customer.

The program should then find out how many banknotes or coins of different values should be returned.

Amount to be paid:
£6.44

Amount Received:
£10.00

Change
3 X £1 Coins
1 X 50p Coin
3 X 2p Coins

Learning Objectives:

By completing this project you will learn how to combine loops and "if statements" effectively to solve a numerical problem.

Tip:

Your program will accept banknotes of £20, £10 and £5 and the following coins: £2, £1, 50p, 20p, 10p. 5p, 2p, 1p.

Extension:

Add some validation rules to ensure that the user has entered valid currency values. You should also check that the amount received from the customer is greater, or equal to, the amount to be paid.

Level of Difficulty: **intermediate** ★★

Python

Bowling Scoreboard

Computing Challenge

Write a little program that prompts the user to enter how many pins they knocked over after each throw.

The program should automatically calculate the total score taking into consideration spares and strikes.

Tip:
Not sure how points are being calculated when playing bowling? Do some research on the Internet to find out!

Learning Objectives:
You will use your Python skills to perform some basic mathematical operations using the input from the end-user. You will understand the need to convert user inputs into integers before using them in mathematical operations.

Extension:
Use file manipulation techniques to write the score into a text file as the game progresses so that the user can keep track of their previous games.

Level of Difficulty: intermediate ★★

Python

Had a look ☐   Work in progress ☐   Nailed it! ☐

Random Name Picker

Computing Challenge

Store the name of your class mates in a text file, one name per line!

Write a little computer program that reads the file and randomly displays one name from the list.

When the name has been picked once, it cannot be picked a second time unless the program is restarted.

Level of Difficulty: **intermediate** ★★

Learning Objectives:
You will learn how to read and retrieve specific information from a text file and to store it using a list.

You will use different techniques to manipulate lists in Python: For instance you will learn how to add and remove entries from a list.

Tip:
To generate random numbers you may want to import the "random" Python library by adding the following command at the beginning of your code:

import random

Python

Birthday Reminder

Computing Challenge

Store information about all your friends in a text file, one friend per line, as follows:

Forename,Surname,Date of Birth

Write a little program that reads the file and tells you whose birthdays to celebrate today!

Level of Difficulty: **intermediate**

Context:

Most computer programs or games need to store and retrieve saved information. This is the case for instance to store your progress or recent scores in a video game. This information can be stored using text files or using more advanced databases.

Learning Objectives:

You will learn how to read and retrieve specific information from a text file.

Extension:

Could your program inform you of all the coming birthdays for the next seven days?

My Sorting Algorithm

Computing Challenge

Store information about all your friends in a text file, one friend per line, as follows:

Forename,Surname,Date of Birth

Write a little program that reads the file and displays the full list of friends sorted in alphabetical order (forename, surname) or in descending order of date of birth.

Learning Objectives:
Insertion Sort, Selection Sort, Bubble Sort, Shell Sort, Merge Sort, Heap Sort, Quick Sort.... There are various methods that can be used to sort data in numerical or alphabetical order. Do some research on the Internet first to investigate and compare these different methods.

Tip:
Some websites such as www.sorting-algorithms.com will help you understand some of the most common sorting algorithms.

Extensions:
Try to solve this challenge by implementing several methods.

Level of Difficulty: **intermediate** ★★

Challenge #62

Multiple Choice Quiz

Computing Challenge

Create a multiple choice quiz where the end-user is asked questions with three possible answers for each question. Only one answer should be correct. The user completes the quiz and gets a total score at the end.

Extension: Amend your script so that the quiz (questions and answers) is stored in a text file so that it's easy to add new questions or edit/remove existing questions.

Learning Objectives:

By completing this challenge you will investigate different forms of user interactions using either a command prompt (text-based user interface) or a Graphical User Interface using graphics and form controls.

Extension:

This extension task consists of reading the questions from a text file. You may want to investigate using XML to format your text file as it gives more options than standard CSV files (Comma Separated Values).

Level of Difficulty: **advanced** ★★★

Python

Had a look ☐   Work in progress ☐   Nailed it! ☐

Simon Says

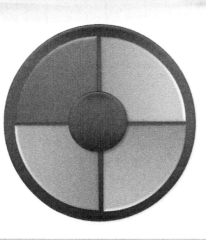

Computing Challenge

Create a computer program that lights up one or more of the four coloured buttons of the "Simon's Disc" in a random order. The player has to reproduce the same sequence by pressing the buttons in order.

As the game progresses, the number of buttons to be pressed increases until the player makes a mistake.

Level of Difficulty: **advanced** ★★★

Learning Objectives:
By completing this project you will create a Graphical User Interface (GUI) and write code to interact with the GUI.

Tip:
To create the user interface you may want to import the PyGame library. Find out more on: http://www.pygame.org

Extension:
Add sound effects each time a button is lit or pressed.

Using a text file, store the score of each player and offer an option to view the leader board displaying te best ten scores.

Sudoku

Computing Challenge

Create a Sudoku Grid that the end-user can complete, one cell at a time.

Each time the user enters a value, the program should check if the grid is valid:

A grid is invalid if the same digit (between 1 and 9) appears more than once on the same row, the same column or the same 3x3 block.

SUDOKU

7		6		1				4
8		5			2	8		9
4		7	6		5	1		7
		1	9					
5				8	6	3		3
1		9						4
4								8

Level of Difficulty: **advanced** ★★★

Did You Know?

Arrays are an effective way to store a collection of values. A list is an array of one dimension. In Python you can create "lists of lists" which are an alternative to multi-dimensional arrays. Do some research on the Internet to find out more about multi-dimensional arrays and how these could help you solve this challenge.

Learning Objectives:

By completing this project you will learn how to loop through the different values of a two-dimensional array.

Morse Code Encoder

Computing Challenge

Create a computer program or webpage where the end-user enters a text message and then presses a button to convert it into Morse code using the ─ (underscore) and . (dot) characters. The computer program will then play the matching sound sequence using on/off tones.

Level of Difficulty: **advanced**

Letter	Code	Letter	Code	Number	Code
A	.-	B	-...	0	-----
C	-.-.	D	-..	1	.----
E	.	F	..-.	2	..---
G	--.	H	....	3	...--
I	..	J	.---	4	....-
K	-.-	L	.-..	5	.....
M	--	N	-.	6	-....
O	---	P	.--.	7	--...
Q	--.-	R	.-.	8	---..
S	...	T	-	9	----.
U	..-	V	...-		
W	.--	X	-..-		
Y	-.--	Z	--..		

S O S

Did You Know?

In Morse code each character is represented by a unique sequence of dots and dashes. The duration of a dash is three times the duration of a dot. Each dot or dash is followed by a short silence, equal to the dot duration. The letters of a word are separated by a space equal to three dots (one dash), and the words are separated by a space equal to seven dots.

Learning Objectives:

This challenge focuses on string manipulation and the creation of basic sound effects.

Extension:

Offer an option to generate and save a .wav file of the sound sequence.

Python

Encrypted Message #1

Did You Know?

In cryptography, a Caesar cipher, also known as Caesar's cipher, the shift cipher, Caesar's code or Caesar shift, is one of the simplest and most widely known encryption techniques. It is a type of substitution cipher in which each letter in the plain text is replaced by a letter some fixed number of positions down the alphabet. For example, with a left shift of 3, D would be replaced by A, E would become B, and so on. The method is named after Julius Caesar, who used it in his private correspondence nearly 2000 years ago!

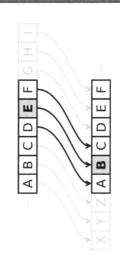

Example of

Caesar's cipher

Computing Challenge

Use a computer algorithm to decrypt the following secret message based on a substitution cipher encryption technique called Caesar's cipher.

Secret Message:

LEJLSSLUA DVYR, FVB OHCL
KLJVKLK   AOPZ   ZLJYLA
TLZZHNL DPAO ZBJJLZZ!

Level of Difficulty: advanced ★★★

Encrypted Message #2

Challenge #67

Computing Challenge

Use a computer algorithm to decrypt the following secret message.

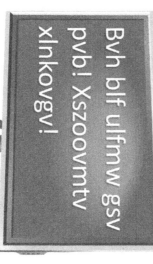

Bvh blf ulfmw gsv
pvb! Xszoovmtv
xlnkovgv!

Did You Know?
Encryption is the process of encoding messages or information in such a way that only authorized parties can read it. Most encryption techniques work on the use of encryption keys. Only those who are aware of the keys can decode encrypted messages.

Encryption techniques are needed to secure information stored on computers or transferred on the Internet. Credit card numbers when you buy online and passwords used to login on websites both need to be encrypted.

For this challenge, we do not give you the key. You need to act as a hacker to decipher this message.

Level of Difficulty: **advanced** ★ ★ ★

Had a look ☐ Work in progress ☐ Nailed it! ☐

Roman Numerals

Did You Know?

Roman Numerals are based on seven symbols:

Symbol	Value
I	1
V	5
X	10
L	50
C	100
D	500
M	1,000

Learning Objectives:

You will fully understand how roman numerals work and you will use mathematical operations and string concatenation to complete this challenge.

Computing Challenge

Create a program that prompts the end-user to enter a number from 1 to 20. The program should then convert this number into a roman numeral.

You can extend this challenge to any number between 1 and 100 or between 1 and 9999!

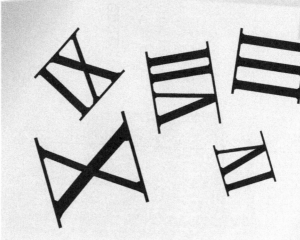

Level of Difficulty: **advanced** ★★★

Python

Decimal/Binary
Converter

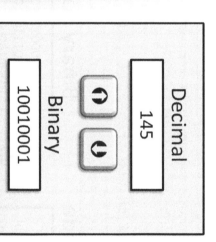

Decimal

145

Binary

10010001

Computing Challenge

Create a computer program that lets you convert any number into binary code.

Tip: Start with numbers between 0 and 255.

Level of Difficulty: **advanced** ★ ★ ★

Did You Know?

Every number between 0 and 255 is made of a unique combination of eight "0's" and "1's".

In binary code, a "bit" is a single digit which can only be 0 or 1. 8 bits form a "Byte".

For instance the binary code for 17 (Decimal) is 00010001.

Learning Objectives:

By completing this challenge you will learn how to convert decimal numbers into binary and vice versa.

Binary Code Encoder

Challenge #70

Computing Challenge

Create a program or a webpage that lets the end-user enter a text message and then press a button to convert it into binary code.

Tip: You will need to use the ASCII code.

Did You Know?
In computing, 1 Byte is made of 8 bits.

Every character on your keyboard has a unique combination of 8 bits. This is based on the ASCII code.

For instance the ASCII code for "A" is 65 which in binary is 01000001

Learning Objectives:
You will learn how to to use the ASCII code to convert textual information into binary code. This is how computers store all your text-based or word-processed computer files.

Text to Encode

There are 10 types of people in the world:
Those who understand binary,
and those who don't.

Binary Code

```
01010100011010001
10010101110100110
01010010000011000
01011100100110101
00100000001100100
11000000100000111
01000111001011100
```

Level of Difficulty: advanced   ★ ★ ★

Minesweeper

Challenge #71

Computing Challenge

Create a 12 by 12 Minesweeper game. The computer should randomly place 20 mines.

The end-user should be able to select a cell (by entering a reference such as A4) to either reveal the number of mines around or "walk over a mine" which ends the game.

Learning Objectives:
By completing this project you will use all of your Python skills to create a fully working and addictive game.

Extension:
Add a stopwatch timer, so that the player has a limited amount of time to complete the game.

Add different levels. Each level will use a different size of grid.

You May Also...
By completing this project as a webpage (HTML/CSS/JavaScript) you will investigate the use of arrays in both JavaScript and in HTML to display the grid.

Level of Difficulty: **advanced** ★★★

Had a look ☐   Work in progress ☐   Nailed it! ☐

Snake Game

Computing Challenge

Write a program to complete the snake game.

The user should be able to control the snake using the arrow keys.

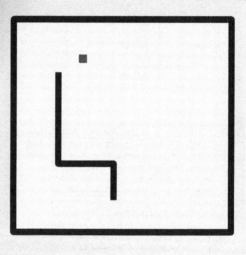

Learning Objectives:

By completing this project you will apply all of your Python skills to complete this retro arcade game which originates from the 1970's. This game became more popular once it became the standard pre-loaded game on Nokia mobile phones in 1998.

Extension:

Create a two-player game using two snakes on the same screen. The players will control their snakes using either the arrow keys or the W,A,S,D keys. The first player to reach the red dot scores a point.

Level of Difficulty: advanced   ★ ★ ★

Battleships

Computing Challenge

Create a computer game of Battleships with a 10x10 grid where the player plays against the computer.

There should be:

⇒ 1 aircraft carrier (5 long),

⇒ 1 battleship (4 long),

⇒ 2 submarines (3 long),

⇒ 1 destroyer (3 long),

⇒ 2 patrol boats (2 long).

Level of Difficulty: **advanced**   ★ ★ ★

Learning Objectives:
By completing this project you will manipulate a two-dimensional array to store the position of the ships on the grid.

Tip:
To create a two-dimensional array in Python you may want to create a list of lists. Do some research on the Internet to see how this would work.

Extension:
Add animation and sound effects each time a ship is hit.

Challenge #73

Mastermind

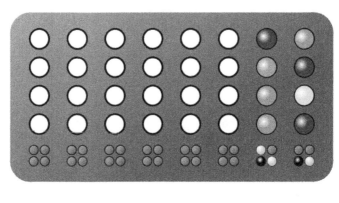

Learning Objectives:

By completing this project you will apply all your Python skills to create a challenging game where the player plays against the computer. You will use a Python library (e.g. PyGame) to create the user interface.

Rules of the Game:

Not too sure about the rules of this game? Check it online by Googling: "Mastermind rules".

Extension:

Let the user choose a combination of four colours and write a programme to see if the computer can play the game to guess the combination using a maximum of ten guesses!

Computing Challenge

Write a program where the end-users have to guess a combination of four colours randomly selected by the computer. The user has ten guesses.

After each guess the computer tells the user how many good pegs or misplaced pegs they have guessed.

Level of Difficulty: **advanced**

★★★

Othello

Challenge
#75

Computing Challenge

Write a program where the end-users plays the game of Othello (aka Reversi) against the computer.

To place a token, the player enters the reference e.g. **A4**.

The computer should decide what is the best place to put its token by evaluating every single available option.

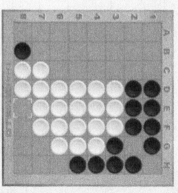

Level of Difficulty: **advanced**   ★ ★ ★

Learning Objectives:
By completing this project you will apply all your Python skills to create a challenging two-player game.

Did You Know?
This game is also known as "Reversi".

If you are not sure how to play this game, check for some instructions on Google.

Tip:
Start by writing the program for two players. This will enable you to focus on the user interface and on applying the rules of the game. Once done, add a routine to let the computer evaluate every possible square to place a token and decide which is the best one to play.

Digital Artist

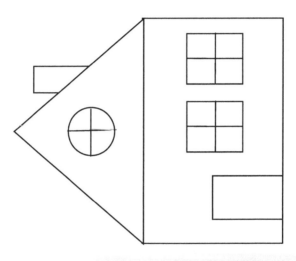

Computing Challenge

Use either Scratch instructions (including "Pen Up" and "Pen Down") or a Python program (using the turtle library) to make a complex drawing.

Try drawing your house, a Christmas tree, a robot or a spaceship.

Learning Objectives:

By completing this project you will learn how to use coordinates to position your cursor on the screen (using x and y coordinates) and how to use basic instructions such as

⇒ *Go To x=0 y=0*
⇒ *Pen Up*
⇒ *Pen Down*
⇒ *Move 10 steps*
⇒ *Turn 90 degrees*
⇒ *Clear*
⇒ *Set Pen Color to...*

You May Also...

Should you wish to complete this challenge using Python, you should investigate using the turtle library.

Find out more on http://docs.python.org/2/library/turtle.html

Level of Difficulty: **beginner**

Starry Night Sky

Computing Challenge

Write a script in Scratch to generate a night sky filled in with stars of different sizes. Each time you run the script the night sky should look different (Random position and sizes for stars)

Level of Difficulty: **beginner** ★

Learning Objectives:
This challenge focuses on some of the techniques learned in the previous challenge (#76: Digital Artist). You will combine these skills with control blocks such as *repeat* to draw multiple stars on the screen. You will also use random numbers on Scratch to get the stars to be randomly positioned on the screen and to be of different sizes.

Tip:
Try the following script to get you started...

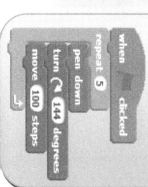

Scratch

Game of It!

Computing Challenge

Create a Scratch game for two players. One player is chasing the other player. When it touches it says:

"You're it!"

Both players should use the keyboard to control their sprite.

Level of Difficulty: **beginner** ★

Learning Objectives:

By completing this project you will learn how to create a two-player game by using two different sprites. You will learn how to make your sprites respond to different key strokes.

Did You Know?

Most computers use a QWERTY keyboard. However, in France, Belgium and some African countries, computers use AZERTY keyboards. This means that the order of the letters on the keyboard is different. In this case, the equivalent of the W, A, S, D keys for an AZERTY keyboard would be Z, Q, S, D!

Challenge
#79

Catch Me If You Can

Computing Challenge

Create a Scratch game where the end-user controls a sprite (burglar) by moving their mouse on the screen (The sprite will walk in the direction of the cursor).

Three policemen should be chasing the sprite automatically.

The game ends when one of the policemen touches the burglar.

Learning Objectives:
By completing this project you will learn how to control a sprite using the mouse cursor instead of the arrow keys.

Extension:
Add gold coins, randomly placed on the screen. The burglar increases his score by collecting these coins. To complete this extension task you will need to create a new variable called "score".

Scratch

Magical Maze

Computing Challenge

Create a Scratch maze where the player controls a sprite using the arrow keys.

The player should collect gold coins to score extra points.

When the player reaches the exit a new maze should be displayed.

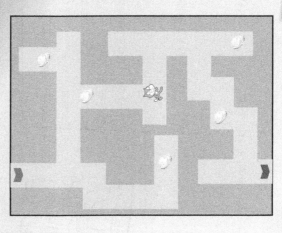

Level of Difficulty: **beginner** ★

Learning Objectives:

To complete this challenge you will need to create your own backdrop for the stage. You can either design it using the built-in Scratch Graphic editor or you can create the stage using your own graphic package and then import it into Scratch.

To create additional levels you will create more backdrops for the stage and use the *switch backdrop* block in your script to move from one level to the other.

Tip:

You can prevent your sprite from "walking through the walls" of your maze by using a *"For ever if / touching colour..."* instruction.

Catch the Fruit

Challenge #81

Computing Challenge

The player controls a basket at the bottom of the screen using either arrows or the mouse pointer. Pieces of fruit are falling randomly from the top. The player scores 1 point for each piece of fruit that falls into the basket.

Level of Difficulty: **intermediate** ★★

Learning Objectives:
By completing this project you will apply all of your Scratch skills to complete one of the most famous arcade games from the 1980's!

Extension:
Turn this game into an educational game. Fruit vs. Vegetable or Healthy vs. Unhealthy food. Each time the player catches a healthy ingredient/snack they score 1 point, each time they catch an unhealthy snack they loose 3 points.

Make sure that the pieces of fruit start falling quicker as the game progresses so that it becomes more and more challenging.

Choose Your Own

Adventure Story

Computing Challenge

Create a "choose your own adventure" story where it is up to the reader to decide where the main character will go. Options should appear on the screen and the user should click on buttons or type answers to decide where to go. The main character should navigate through several rooms or landscapes and interact with other characters/sprites.

> Would you like to go right or left?

Learning Objectives:

By completing this challenge you will investigate different approaches that can be used to interact with sprites. Your main sprite will ask questions, receive answers typed by the end-user and use them to control the flow of the game. You may also enable the user to click on other sprites to interact with them or to move the main sprite around.

Tip:

Make sure you get one of your friends to test your game. They may find a bug that you will have to fix and will give you some valuable feedback to help you improve your game further.

Level of Difficulty: intermediate ★★

Car Racing Game

Computing Challenge

Create a car racing game for two players.

Both players should use the keyboard to control their own car which should be slowed down when they drive off the track.

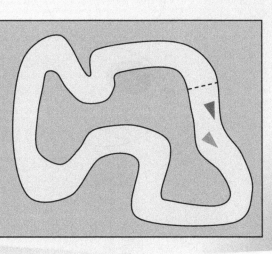

Learning Objectives:
By completing this project you will learn how to create a two-player game by using two different sprites. You will learn how to make your sprites respond to different key strokes and interact with the background.

Tip:
Use the up and down keys to control the speed of the car and left and right arrow keys to control its direction/angle.

Extension:
Investigate the use of variables to store the amount of laps completed by each player.

Level of Difficulty: **intermediate** ★★

Challenge #84

Rolling Eyes

Learning Objectives:

There are several ways to interact and control a sprite in Scratch. Some of the previous challenges looked at using the arrow keys to control the sprite. This challenge looks at how the mouse pointer can be used to control the sprite.

For this challenge you will have to design your own sprite to draw the pupil of the eyes.

Extension:

Use different costumes to make your eyes blink when the user clicks on the mouse.

Is it possible to respond to left and right click of the mouse to decide which eye should blink?

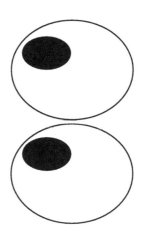

Computing Challenge

Draw two eyes in Scratch and get them to follow the position of your mouse pointer on the screen.

Level of Difficulty: intermediate ★★

Digital to Analogue
Clock Converter

Computing Challenge

Write a program that lets the end-users enter a time in digital format (e.g. 3.53pm).

The program will display an analogue clock displaying the time entered by the end-user.

Learning Objectives:
You will define your own variables and use some mathematical calculations in Scratch. You will use these variables to rotate your sprites (hands of the clock).

Tip:
You will complete some cross-multiplication to convert a time into an angle.

The little hand turns around the clock (360°) in 12 hours, and the big hand turns around the clock in 60 minutes.

Level of Difficulty: **advanced**   ★ ★ ★

Pacman

Computing Challenge

Create a game of Pacman where the end-user can control the Pacman sprite using the arrow keys on the keyboard.

To keep it simple you may want to have ghosts that can walk through the walls or move randomly throughout the maze without actually chasing Pacman.

Learning Objectives:

By completing this project you will apply all of your Scratch skills to complete one of the most famous arcade games from the 1980's!

Tip:

You may want to reuse some of the scripts that you created for challenge #80: Magical Maze.

Extension:

Make sure that the user has three lives to start with.

Add special pac-dots that enable Pacman to become invincible for 10 seconds.

Once Pacman has eaten all the pac-dots, he should start on the next level with a new maze.

Level of Difficulty: **advanced**

Pong

Scratch

Had a look ☐   Work in progress ☐   Nailed it! ☐

Computing Challenge

Create a Scratch game of Pong for two players.

Both players should use the keyboard to control their own bat/sprite.

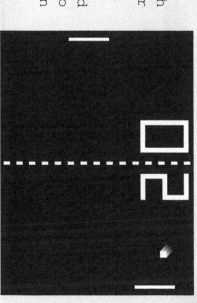

Learning Objectives:
By completing this project you will apply all of your Scratch skills to complete one of the most famous arcade games from the 1980's!

Extension:
Add an extra mode where the player can play against the computer!

You May Also...
Try to create this game using Python. You will need to use a library such as the PyGame library to build the interface.

Scratch

Breakout Game

Learning Objectives:
By completing this project you will apply all of your Scratch or Python skills to complete this classic game from the 1980's!

Extension:
Add different levels with different patterns of blocks. Use different types of blocks including blocks that need to be hit twice to disappear.

Storing Your Scores:
Use a text file to store your scores and display a top ten best scores screen at the beginning of the game. You can use this extension for all your computer games!

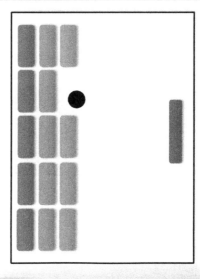

Computing Challenge

Create a breakout game.

The user should have three lives.

Extra options should appear/fall down when you break some of the blocks: wider spaceship, two balls, faster/slower ball, extra life etc.

Level of Difficulty: **advanced** ★ ★ ★

Space Invaders

Computing Challenge

Create a Scratch game of Space Invaders.

The player should control their spaceship using the arrow keys on the keyboard and the space bar to shoot the invaders.

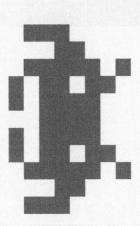

Level of Difficulty: **advanced**   ★ ★ ★

Learning Objectives:
By completing this project you will apply all of your Scratch skills to complete one of the most famous arcade games from the 1980's!

Extension:
Allow space invaders to randomly shoot towards the end-user space ships and add a number of lives.

You May Also...
Try to create this game using Python. You will need to use a library such as the PyGame library to build the interface.

Had a look ☐   Work in progress ☐   Nailed it! ☐

Scratch

Flappy Bird

challenge **#90**

Computing Challenge

Create a Scratch game of Flappy Bird.

The player should use the space bar to control the flappy bird and score 1 point every time the bird passes through the green tubes.

Level of Difficulty: **advanced** ★★★

Learning Objectives:

By completing this project you will apply all of your Scratch skills to complete a "best selling" game! You will use a trial and error approach to fine-tune your game to make it fun and challenging.

There are many parameters to adapt the level of difficulty of this game: size of the bird, speed of the tubes, size of the gaps between the tubes, width of the tubes, strength of the "flap" and of the gravity, space between the tubes etc. You will find the right balance between all of these parameters. You can also design different levels or make the game become harder as the score increases.

Angry Tanks

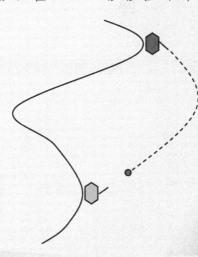

Computing Challenge

This is a two-player game. Each player controls a tank. They can choose the angle and the power they want to use before shooting.

The projectile should follow a parabola trajectory based on the chosen angle and power of the shoot.

Level of Difficulty: **advanced** ★★★

Did You Know?
There are several variations of this game such as Worms or, more recently, Angry Birds.

Learning Objectives:
By completing this project you will apply all of your Scratch skills to complete one of the most famous retro artillery games from the 1980's!

You May Also...
Try to create this game using Python. You will need to use a library such as the PyGame library to build the interface.

Scratch

Tetris

Computing Challenge

Create a game of Tetris based on the following pieces:

Learning Objectives:
Apply all of your skills to complete this challenging game.

Extension:
Add different levels by changing the speed of the game (how fast the bricks are moving).

You May Also...
Try to create this game using Python. You will need to use a library such as the PyGame library to build the interface.

Level of Difficulty: **advanced** ★★★

Top Trumps

Computing Challenge

Create a Top Trumps table using Database Software to store the information that appears on the Top Trumps Cards.

Create a form to easily create new cards, and a report to print your Top Trumps cards.

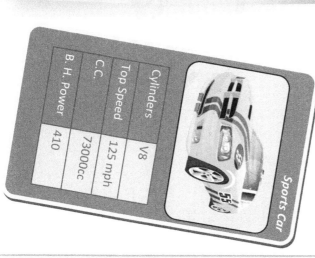

Sports Car

Cylinders	V8
Top Speed	125 mph
C.C.	73000cc
B. H. Power	410

Context:

Databases provide a very effective way to store all sorts of information on any topic. Most interactive websites are using databases to store user profiles, orders, site access statistics, posts etc.

Learning Objectives:

You will learn how to create a single table using appropriate fields. You will also input data into your table. Each card of the game will be stored as one record. Finally you will learn how to display the data from your table in a more visual way by using a report.

Database

Had a look ☐ Work in progress ☐ Nailed it! ☐

Solar System DB

Challenge #94

Computing Challenge

Create a database about the solar system, storing as much information as you can find about each planet.

Create a "Planets" table and choose the right field name, data type and field size for each field.

Level of Difficulty: **beginner** ★

Learning Objectives:
You will learn how to create a single table using appropriate fields. You will investigate the use of various data types including text, number (integer or real), boolean, date and time.

When using text fields you will consider the field size (maximum number of characters) to be allocated for each field to optimise the file size of the database.

Did you know:
The maximum field size of a text field is 255 characters. Sometimes you may need to store long descriptions and do not want a maximum number of characters. In this case you can use a "memo" (aka Blob) data type.

My MP3 Playlists

Computing Challenge

Create a database to store information about all of your mp3's, albums and favourite artists.

Create a user interface using forms and reports to view all the songs from a specific artist or band, or from a specific album, and add or edit songs, artists or albums' details.

Create a "Playlist" table to organise your favourite tracks into various playlists.

Level of Difficulty: **intermediate** ★★

Context:
Most databases are used to store information about multiple entities. In this instance the database will save information about MP3 Tracks but also about Bands/Artists and about albums.

Learning Objectives:
You will learn how to create a relational database using multiple tables and how to create relationships between these tables. You will learn about the use of primary keys and foreign keys in a database.

Football League Table

Computing Challenge

Create a database to store information about all the football teams in the Premier league.

The database should also be used to store results of games being played.

Using this information, create a report to show a complete league table with automatic calculation of the total number of matches played by each team and the total number of points for each team.

Learning Objectives:

Once the data is stored within data tables, queries can be used to manipulate, filter and sort the records. Reports can also be created to display information in various formats and calculated fields can be used to perform mathematical operations.

Extension:

If you are a football fan you can extend this model further and include a "Football Players" table, a "Referees" table, a "stadia" table, and link these tables to other tables in your database.

Level of Difficulty: **intermediate** ★★

My e-Shop

Challenge #97

Computing Challenge

Create a database to store information about items you would like to sell, users of the database and their orders.

Each user should be able to buy more than one item per order. For each item, they should be able to change the required quantity.

Create an input form that lets the user complete an order by selecting various items and quantities. The form should automatically calculate the total cost of the order. Tip: look at online shopping baskets to see how your order form should work.

Level of Difficulty: **advanced** ★★★

Context:

Nearly all web2.0 websites use back-end databases to store the information displayed on the website. This is the case for search engines, social networks, blogs, and e-commerce websites (online shops).

Learning Objectives:

You will understand how e-commerce websites store information about their products, customers and orders using a relational database. You will use calculated forms and calculated forms with multiple items/lines sub forms with calculated fields to create a shopping basket user interface.

My eBay Database

Computing Challenge

Create a database to store information about items to be sold, users, and their bids.

Create a user interface using forms and reports to enable sellers to add items, see the items they have sold, and for buyers to bid on items and see what items they have purchased.

All items will need a start and end date and time, for buyers to be able to bid on these items.

Learning Objectives:

By completing this challenge you will investigate how information stored by auction websites can be structured in a relational database. You will apply all your database skills to create the data tables and the relationships between the entities of your database. You will create various reports using complex queries.

Extension:

What other functionalities do websites like eBay offer? (Buyer/Seller Rating, eBay Shops, Advanced Search, Watch Lists, Buy Now option etc.)

Level of Difficulty: **advanced**   ★★★

Database

My Family Tree

Challenge #99

Computing Challenge

Create a database to store basic information (Forename, Surname, Gender, DoB) about all your family members and how they relate to each other.

Build some complex queries to answer some specific questions such as:

⇒ Who are all the siblings of a family member?

⇒ Have they got any nephews or nieces?

⇒ What are the names of their parents?

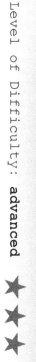

Level of Difficulty: **advanced** ★★★

Learning Objectives:
Relational databases can be used to store most models but may not be ideal to store trees (e.g. family trees, folder or structures). Though Hierarchical databases or Graph databases would be more appropriate, this challenge looks at how to store a family tree using a relational database. Do some research online. You may find different solutions for this challenge. Put them to the test by setting up the queries to answer the given questions.

My Social Network

Computing Challenge

Create a database to store information about members (profiles), friendships and posts.

Each user should be able to update their profile, add/remove friends and post feeds.

Each user should have a report called "My Wall" where they can see their own posts and the posts of all their friends in chronological order.

Each user should also be able to see their list of friends and click on these to access their profile.

Learning Objectives:
By completing this challenge you will design an Entity Relational Diagram for a complex scenario. You will evaluate the impacts that the ERD has on the functionalities of the application.

Further Reading:
Relational databases have their limitations especially when the volume of data and connected users increases significantly (as this is the case for large social networks). Other models can be used. Find out more by researching the web about distributed databases, database replication, push and pull models or Graph databases.

Level of Difficulty: **advanced** ★★★

HTML/CSS

JavaScript

Python

Scratch

Database

Challenge #101

Challenge #101

Computing Challenge

Challenge #101 is for you to define your own challenge or project.

Decide what you are going to do, define the rules of your next game, decide what technology your are going to use or learn about.

Fancy learning a new programming language? Want to learn how to create a responsive website? Want to design your own App? The possibilities are endless...

Be creative, be ambitious, be resourceful and enjoy the process!

Challenge Yourself...
You can reuse most of the challenges from this book using a different programming language. For instance you can try to complete some of the Scratch games in Python or as a webpage using JavaScript.

Find Out More...
Visit www.101computing.net to find more resources to help you with these challenges as well as new challenges for you to investigate.

Reference

#	Challenge	HTML	JavaScript	Python	Scratch	Database	Beginner	Intermediate	Advanced
1	Hello World	✔	✔	✔	✔		✔		
2	My First HTML Page	✔					✔		
3	10-Tag Challenge	✔					✔		
4	My Timetable	✔					✔		
5	My Online Survey	✔					✔		
6	My Photo Collage	✔					✔		
7	Where on the Map?	✔					✔		
8	My FavIcon.ico	✔					✔		
9	Bookmark Me!	✔					✔		
10	My Popups	✔					✔		
11	Web Clock	✔					✔		
12	My Widgets	✔					✔		
13	My CSS layout	✔						✔	
14	My Responsive CSS Layout	✔							✔
15	My CSS Text Frames	✔						✔	
16	My Tabs	✔						✔	
17	Roll-over QR Codes	✔						✔	
18	My School Map	✔						✔	
19	My Splash Screen	✔						✔	
20	Quote Scroller	✔							✔
21	My Image Gallery	✔							✔
22	Pull Down Menus	✔							✔
23	Google Fonts	✔							✔
24	My Colour Palette		✔				✔		
25	Guess the Colour		✔				✔		
26	What's the Time in New-York?		✔	✔			✔		

#	Challenge	HTML	JavaScript	Python	Scratch	Database	Beginner	Intermediate	Advanced
27	Christmas Countdown		✔	✔			✔		
28	Daily Greetings		✔	✔			✔		
29	Quote of the Day		✔	✔			✔		
30	Word Count		✔	✔			✔		
31	On Which Day of the Week Were You Born?		✔	✔			✔		
32	My Countdown Timer		✔	✔				✔	
33	Form Validation		✔					✔	
34	Captcha		✔					✔	
35	Paper Size		✔	✔				✔	
36	My Calculator		✔	✔				✔	
37	How Secure is Your Password?		✔	✔				✔	
38	Currency Converter		✔	✔				✔	
39	How Fast Can You Type?		✔	✔					✔
40	#Hex / RGB Colour Converter		✔	✔					✔
41	My Texting App		✔	✔					✔
42	Memory Game		✔	✔					✔
43	Tic-Tac-Toe		✔	✔					✔
44	Connect4		✔	✔					✔
45	Hangman		✔	✔					✔
46	Adding from 1 to 100		✔	✔			✔		
47	My Average Score		✔	✔			✔		
48	Guess the Number		✔	✔			✔		
49	Prime Number Check		✔	✔			✔		
50	Poker Dice		✔	✔			✔		
51	What's my Age?		✔	✔			✔		
52	Backwards Writing		✔	✔			✔		
53	It's all in the Case		✔	✔				✔	
54	Random Password Generator		✔	✔				✔	
55	Love Match Calculator		✔	✔				✔	
56	Darts Scoreboard		✔	✔				✔	

#	Challenge	HTML	JavaScript	Python	Scratch	Database	Beginner	Intermediate	Advanced
57	What's My Change?		✔	✔				✔	
58	Bowling Scoreboard		✔	✔				✔	
59	Random Name Picker			✔				✔	
60	Birthday Reminder			✔				✔	
61	My Sorting Algorithm			✔				✔	
62	Multiple Choice Quiz			✔					✔
63	Simon Says			✔					✔
64	Sudoku			✔					✔
65	Morse Code Encoder			✔					✔
66	Encrypted Message #1			✔					✔
67	Encrypted Message #2			✔					✔
68	Roman Numerals			✔					✔
69	Decimal/Binary Converter			✔					✔
70	Binary Code Encoder			✔					✔
71	Minesweeper			✔					✔
72	Snake Game			✔					✔
73	Battleships			✔					✔
74	Mastermind			✔					✔
75	Othello			✔					✔
76	Digital Artist			✔	✔		✔		
77	Starry Night Sky			✔	✔		✔		
78	Game of It!			✔	✔		✔		
79	Catch Me If You Can			✔	✔		✔		
80	Magical Maze			✔	✔		✔		
81	Catch the Fruit			✔	✔			✔	
82	Choose Your Own Adventure Story			✔	✔			✔	
83	Car Racing Game			✔	✔			✔	
84	Rolling Eyes			✔	✔			✔	
85	Digital to Analogue Clock Converter			✔	✔				✔
86	Pacman			✔	✔				✔

#	Challenge	HTML	JavaScript	Python	Scratch	Database	Beginner	Intermediate	Advanced
87	Pong			✔	✔				✔
88	Breakout Game			✔	✔				✔
89	Space Invaders			✔	✔				✔
90	Flappy Bird			✔	✔				✔
91	Angry Tanks			✔	✔				✔
92	Tetris			✔	✔				✔
93	Top Trumps					✔	✔		
94	Solar System DB					✔	✔		
95	My MP3 Playlists					✔		✔	
96	Football League Table					✔		✔	
97	My e-Shop					✔			✔
98	My eBay Database					✔			✔
99	My Family Tree					✔			✔
100	My Social Network					✔			✔
101	Challenge #101	✔	✔	✔	✔	✔	✔	✔	✔

Lightning Source UK Ltd.
Milton Keynes UK
UKOW06f1249181115

262994UK00020B/689/P